Selenity Book Four

Selenity Book Four

New Poems by
Richard Fenton Sederstrom

Published by the Jackpine Writers' Bloc, Inc.

Copyright © 2016 Richard Fenton Sederstrom
All rights reserved

Published by the Jackpine Writers' Bloc, Inc.
Edited by Sharon Harris
Layout and cover design by Tarah L. Wolff
Moon Photographs by Richard Fenton Sederstrom

$15.00
978-1-928690-32-0

Selenity Book Four

Dedication

This book is for Carol, my love, my dearest companion, and my eyes, and for Nick Salerno, my oldest friend, my teacher, and my conscience.

And for my children, my grandchildren and my great-grandchildren.

And beyond to those descendant promises—who may live their lives on a planet . . . : Ah, that they may live their lives, and that they may do so on a planet that can be lived on.

Also, for the fifth book so far, to Sharon Harris and Tarah L. Wolff for their continuing forbearance and their growing professionalism and artistry dealing with the confusions of my typescripts and the piffle of the poet.

Also by Richard Fenton Sederstrom

Fall Pictures on an Abandoned Road

Disordinary Light

Folly, A Book of Last Summers

Eumaeus Tends

Acknowledgments

A special acknowledgment to the young poets whose work is printed either whole or in excerpt at the end of "Codex, A Case for the Lonely Poet." These are:

Enrique Garcia Naranjo, "Guadalajara Wash"
Hannah Irene Walsh, "To Want," (excerpt)
Emily Long, "To the Man I Never Knew," (excerpt)
Zoe Keeter, "From My Ghost to Yours," (excerpt)

My sincere wish to each of you for a long and adventurous career in service to humankind's codex. — *RFS*

A word on the title:

About a decade ago, a student quoted in a note to me a not uncommon self-descriptive tag, "Senility is just another word for adventure." Only he spelled the first word "Selenity." A condition of being moon-like? Lunitas? The notion serves me so well that I have used *Selenity* as a working title for my first three books. It is time to give selenity light. Ergo: *Selenity Book Four.*

The author gratefully acknowledges the following anthologies, journals, and magazines for their kind permission to reproduce the following poems:

The Blue Guitar Magazine: "Anomalopoesis: whiffs of a morning with Garbage," "At Split Rock," "August Afternoon at Play," "A Capitalist," "Cell Phone," "Charon's Choo Choo," "A Child," "Codex: A Case for the Lonely Poet," "A Deceit of Old Weather," "Elegy for the Last Iguanodon," "Eumaeus Old Tends to Conveniences," "Fate Motif," "A Grace from the Usurer," "Grandmothers on Tour," "An Intention," "The Little Bang," "Note to the Office of Interpretation," "Notes from M. Arouet," "Of an Age," "The Older," "Orphans in Concordia," "Paper Boy," "Sanctuary," "Some Aspen," "Upsittingly I Am Arranged," "Working Verse around the Green Commons."

Reflections 2013: A Yearbook of the Citizens Lake and Stream Monitoring Programs (Minnesota Pollution Control Agency): "Loonshine."

Dissident Voice: "Alice Among the Wonders," "The Becoming," "Families on Streets in Cities," "*La Plume d'Anthropocène,*" "Lines Too Lonely to Find Their Poem," "The Newly Risen," "Surprise, Surprise," "Waiting for the Tweet of Doom."

The Talking Stick: "Fall Harvest," "Family Chat," "Glare," "Residuaries."

Unstrung: "After Wards: a Disconstruction of Future Reflection," "Climate Cha[lle]nge," "It Might Be Nice if We Brought Flowers," "Notes in Black and White," "Soliloquy by the Candle Light of Day," "Tourist as Shaman, Shaman as Tourist."

Contents

Part One: Phases and Settings

Waxing Full
An Intention 5
Some Aspen 6
Charon's Choo-Choo 7
At Split Rock 9
Grandmothers on Tour 10
Family Chat 12
Sanctuary 13
Toward the Horn Gate 14
Paper Boy 15
Man with Crow 16
Gray and Scant 17
Of an Age 18

Glow on Water
Fate Motif 23
A Deceit of Old Weather 26
Climate Cha[lle]nge 27
Residuaries 28
Glare 29
Loonshine 30
Cold and Bright, the View from Below 31
Fall Harvest 32
Notes in Black and White 33
Badlands 34
Lucretius' Dervish 35
August Afternoon at Play 36
"It Might Be Nice if We Brought Flowers" 37
Elegy for the Last Iguanodon 38

Overcast
Upsittingly I Am Arranged 43
Cell Phone 45
"La Plume de" . . . The Candy Wrappers of History 46
A Capitalist 47
Feeding 48
Patriot Two-Step 49
A Grace from the Usurer 50
Life and Dis-Life in the Late Anthropocene 51
Time Scale 53
Eumaeus Old Tends to Conveniences 54
Waiting for the Tweet of Doom 55

Break: Setting at Day-Break
Soliloquy by the Candle Light of Day 59

Part Two: What We Learn, What We Become
For and in memory of Nick Salerno, Magister et Frater

For the Living . . . and the Living
Working Verse around the Green Commons 67
Words with Heraclitus 69
The Newly Risen 72
A Child 74
"O Crustacean" 75
Silence of Echoes in Caves 76
The Little Bang 78
The Older 80
A State of Poise 81
The Becoming 82

Codex, A Case for the Lonely Poet
Codex, A Case for the Lonely Poet 87

Anomalopoesis
After Wards 105
Note to the Office of Interpretation 107
What is seems 108
Lines Too Lonely to Find Their Poem 110
Families on Streets in Cities 113
Alice among the Wonders 115
La Plume d'Anthropocène 116
Lych-Gathering 117
Surprise, Surprise 118
Anomalopoesis: whiffs of a morning with *Garbage* 121
Orphans in Concordia 123
Notes from M. Arouet 126
Tourist as Shaman/Shaman as Tourist 128
Ending After Wards 129

Break: Selene Eos
Måne 135

Endnotes to "A Case for the Lonely Poet" 139

Part One: Phases and Settings

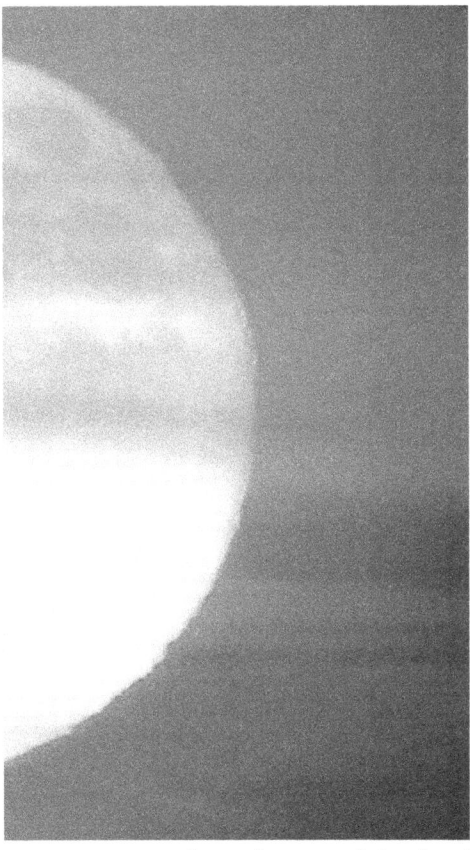

My poems are quiet, so say my several readers, and I ask of readers that they spend contemplative time within and without the poem, any poem, as a way of getting into the conversation. Contemplation is a beneficial occupation, not always—nor necessarily —a happy one, but always worthy—virtuous in the best sense of the word. That most people use their hard-won literacy as machinery is not the poets' fault; we are much too idle (by Whitman's easy standard, we "loaf"), and educated folk assume that they aren't idle. But to assume is to avoid the patterns by which the mind is employed.

Waxing Full

An Intention

that some poem after this might refract
from the ancient energy of a petroglyph
on a rough rock-face in the desert sun

directed by the impervious lines
in the stubble of granite, crude because
of the physics of brother and sister atoms

who make of immovable geology a sexuality
to reflect a purity not of beauty but of
articulate isness perfectly blended

into the script of eons of erosion—
the specific medium for Antelope, Lizard,
Sun-Radiance, Lightning-Bolt—inscriptions,

characters too immediate to the soul for mere beauty
in a language designed to celebrate
the raw abundance of scarcity, of appetite,

a shaman-world of necessary generation,
the apposite ideal of what the pencil and eraser will do
like a ghost to erode the sheet of paper

that reflects the scratches of the written poem,
a grave-rubbing of what cannot erase itself
from lives that can do nothing else.

Some Aspen

Some aspen still
stand, autumn clad
whose third green is also gold.

Birch stand, already
telling in their skeletal
bareness the Hallow-

een fable of winter
dying, the possible
truth we scurry

through and beyond,
those of us who can.
Only the oaks

remain in pure strength,
tans, russets, browns,
leather-clad

or calloused cracked
hands of laborers,
artisans of evolution.

They still conjure
a fable of life in us,
glory of green imagined.

Selenity Book Four

Charon's Choo-Choo

We feel the machine slipping from our hands,
as if someone else were steering;
if we see a light at the end of the tunnel,
it's the light of an oncoming train.
        Robert Lowell, "Since 1939"

Dynee is five. She pushes
her baby brother Stevie in his tin stroller.
Dynee pushes because she is the Mommy.
I am the Daddy because Dynee is the Mommy.
So I run ahead, to get away from Daddy.
My little brother Jackie runs after me
because my little brother Jackie runs after me.

But mostly I run to be the first
at the last street corner we're allowed to run to,
about three blocks from-or-up-or-down Sibley Ave.
And because I am not allowed to run farther
I walk fast for another block, and that takes me
as close to the tracks as I dare let Jackie go.
Somewhere, I go farther. Somewhere I run

to meet the great black locomotive that pushes
out of the vast deep west to meet me.
The great gray solidity of steam hisses
toward me, whistle ready, bell-rope taut,
rolls slower to address my salute. The engine chuffs
its invitation to come aboard and I come aboard.
I feel the cold of iron throttle through a leather palm.

My gloved hands are gauntleted to the elbow.
I check the dials, the clocks to somewhere east
and I jam the throttle lever forward to some
distant early sunrise, times past to when
this locomotive was new that is now obsolete.
Engine burns mine-mountains of gleaming black coal.
Black diamonds sacrificed to the fiery furnace.

> > >

Then it slides past me, and Dynee now
and Stevie and Jackie back at the corner of Sibley.
In the aging mind of another childhood past
I reach into my shorts pocket for three coins—
pennies, two for my eyes, one for the engineer
who waves his hand now palm upward
in the grace of subservience to the deathless fire

or to question:
              maybe my small fate,
      hidden until he raises his palm to halt,
and bids welcome.

Selenity Book Four

At Split Rock
for Carolyn Forché

You're right about Lighthouses, of course.
They are places of "being alone"—
under the vast refractory of prism
through prism upon prism
through year, decade, century, crush of water,
fathom upon fathom upon
the great gray epitome of mud

which lies quiet,
patient while it practices to become in turn
only one among the death-count of strata
that lie as layers of Earth's calloused skin
each layer sometime exposed to the aloneness
of water working us gently warmly
away into the womb of Earth once more—

alone with the shining black orthocone
alone with mosasaur and muskellunge
with the weightless grace of a birch-bark canoe
with the Edmund Fitzgerald
with the fishing boat out there running
in a panicky straight white-knuckled
line against the waves—

with you far beyond my side,
Selene's torch searching out into the night
into the chronometer of beam timing the waves,
the passage of that distant ore freighter
or the fading lights that might be anything very large
and moving very slowly
all alone, save for ourselves and all else.

Grandmothers on Tour

Nana took her only
        tour of Sweden
                some fifty years
     ago.
She returned
        with a photo
            album
      mortuary-packed
with pictures of
        churches, graveyards
              and a hospital
     or two.
In respect and silence
        we followed Nana's
              eschatological
      tour of our future
and we kept our distance.

Babe took a camera
        on one of her
              several ambles
        back to England—
pressed upon her
        by her closest family
              who might
      have remembered
knowing Babe better.

Babe returned with
        dozens of stories—
              places, people,
     the view
of the Spanish Steps,

> > >

Selenity Book Four

              a semi-accidental
                        side trip,
                 and how
          she didn't
                 get the chance
                           in her merry schedule
                 to drop in on the Pope.
          Babe took a single
                 photo: in
                           the London Zoo
                 of an American
          Bison.
                 Our laughter still
                           echoes.
                 Babe's too.

Family Chat

"She's worse," he says, like that,
but not worse than what.
We don't express our feelings much,
or well, around here.

"She's worse.
She's been kind of out of it, these last four days,
so we're taking her to the hospital."
We go back down the hill.

Nancy would have asked what we might want to drink.
"We have some lemonade I think,
and maybe a Coke. Iced tea?
Jim, do we have iced tea?"

"You want a cup of coffee?" he'd ask instead.
"No, thanks." We'd sit on the couch,
answer the annual questions, mostly
about the brothers I've hardly seen in years.

Together we'd intone the memorial to last winter's weather,
"But maybe we'll have snow this year, finally."
We'd shrug in solemn agreement, nod, almost smile,
step out the door again.

Selenity Book Four

Sanctuary
in memory of Barbie Fenton

I have come here for the sun, for the warmth
   of the sun, for the healing clarity and warmth
   of the sun. I am not a sad evacuee.

I have come to the desert for the warmth
   of the sun, for the warmth of the sun
   upon the chill in my consumptive lungs.

Which are clear of all disease, save dis-ease.
   The breath I long for is not only the cure from enveloping
   microbes. The breath I long for is love somewhere

out from the end of enveloping lornness, the chill
   of consumption in my heart, for which
   I have come for the warmth of the sun

in the desert, to which I am not a mere sad
   evacuee. The desert where I am not only here
   to cough up the microbial detritus

of the clotted chill in my consumed heart,
   the unconsummated distance between my heart
   and the horizon of consuming emptiness.

I have come for the empty warmth
   of the consuming desert sun, the chill
   of the consuming lorn horizon. And the sun.

Toward the Horn Gate

In this resolution of small chaos
Penelope has become Telemachus' father.
But what has become of Odysseus?

Loved again, but for what he had been
before, maybe only, maybe
in the shadow of her bridal memory now,

maybe a fading doppelganger,
having passed her test, not she her own,
living now in *her* Ithaca, not his.

Does he become to her a bauble,
a reincarnation of Calypso's
choice and tender morsel?

So loved, does he long already
for the memory yet uncontrived,
the landlocked shade of prophecy carved in ash?

Selenity Book Four

Paper Boy

Because you remember
those kerosene lamps,
the ones we sometimes
played with at road construction
sites in the nights way back then,
that sometimes exploded,
soared into the night—

you may know what it felt like
when I fell off my paper-laden bike,
when the canvas bag
of Cold War intimidations
bounced on the pavement
and the end of a handlebar
punched into my gut.

I didn't think I would
ever breathe again, never
knew before that morning
how much I still enjoy
the explosion of my
second first breath.

Man with Crow
for Hugh Fenton

That old man there
in the frayed
plaid shirt

always walked with Earth,
felt her caress his feet.

Once he bought a talking crow
from a fishing buddy.

The sleek bird
only spoke once
and only in crow.

The man spoke
back in man,
for the return modesty
of honest talk

and let it fly.

Selenity Book Four

Gray and Scant

Hairs gray
and scant insinuate
that the narrow
head (soon to be
adverbially defunct)

may be as empty
inside these days as
the head is clearly
empty outside:
a pocky veneer.

Of an Age

I am of an age when
I cannot be expected to listen
to anything anyone tries to tell me.

So without saying anything
that might interrupt tradition
or expectation I turn my head

and I listen as though
the last moment of my life
depended on every second

I listen. Then in the vast array
of those final seconds
I try to clear from the gently

falling chaff the golden grains
the seeds of ripening memory.
In the tangle of those lines

I grasp that I have informed
myself that these agricultural
efforts often come to naught:

the pedestrian mis-thought
gladdens me however
with a cloud of future in which

I will enter once more upon the tenure
of learning I started inadvertently
those seconds of listening ago.

Selenity Book Four

Glow on Water

Fate Motif

We drift again.
Our boat trolls powerless in a brisk
breeze along a mid-lake shoal toward deep water.

A couple in a green rowboat lies off the rock bar
there to the east of us, far side of the third buoy.
The green boat drifts with us in company with
*

our radio and the first movement of Brahms' First Symphony.
These difficult moments always seem troubled, out of place.
Is it an anguished family argument? Fear the Master?

Is it a shudder of his nervous composing that seems at first
so apart from the Brahms we knew? The shock of distortions
will come later, in memory. The old familiar

of the perfectionist we know and the perfect
calm of confidence we think we share with Brahms
in the music and the peace of our listening.
*

They sit together in that small aluminum boat.
It's one of the green rowboats people who vacation
at Evergreen Lodge rent from Karl Dyre.

They vacation as they have lived for many years.
Together.
Together they slip away from the dock

after he's got the hang, the élève's perfectionist touch,
of the fifteen-horse outboard motor
in a humiliating false note apart, *primo*,

> > >

while he faces the possibility that he hasn't remembered
what Karl had told him again about the choke,
to position the throttle, and be sure it's in neutral.

It is a moment apart for her too, *secondo* for now
because of the problem with the motor—there isn't one—
("O, let him not flood it this time!").

That problem is the state of his apartness
which he shares with her in the distance
she must make of her own apartness . . .

together in the boat, away now from the crowded, summer-heated cabin,
from a tedious daughter-in-law and the grandchildren,
the darlings we miss so when we're apart but, O, the noise sometimes.

Most times.
It's good to be apart now and together in the little green boat.
He baits her hook for her.

And he tells her again how not to snarl the line and maybe
just let the line out and don't try to cast and . . .
O, well.

He baits his own hook and he flips his bait easily into the water.
And they wait. Together. A *due*. But each apart nevertheless,
wondering apart how long before we go back or—*How peaceful* . . .

The poetry of silence reaches them now and the grandchildren.
They make peace with the daughter-in-law,
and we return to the radio, BBC Proms live recording
*

> > >

Selenity Book Four

and hear the audience's fidgety scuffling at the movement's end,
a shudder of nervousness. Out of the audible hum of confusion
someone begins to clap, alone and apart, the Audience Master.

Then a few more take up this faltering acquaintance.
Then maybe most of the audience, and maybe Brahms himself
after all the years before the symphony takes conventional life and leaves
                        *

them to their contented roll in the green rowboat.
And we, worried now over Brahms' baited twisting,
his splenetic apprenticeship as "Tenth Symphony" composer.
                        *

And I am left to dispute with my own despots, who create
the daughter-in-law, the possibilities of peace and my
devious conceit misconstructing these tenuous symphonics.

A Deceit of Old Weather

Is *déjà vu* false *déjà vu*
when the flight of near memory
leads me back to the exact place
and the exact time of the incident *vu*?

Or is the *vue* of that time
and place out of the extraordinary
number of times and places *déjà*?
Does inexactitude make

from false memory true *vue*?

Selenity Book Four

Climate Cha[lle]nge

The lake is green with
probabilities of pollen.

A clam concentrates downward
in its industry of not moving

save for so much occasion as to compact
time into original molecules.

Halves of small shells lie concave to the sun.
They reflect original light.

They wait for the next age of limestone
to mold old death into new Earth.

Residuaries

We reside on the shore surrounding the lake.
We are held here between the forest and the lake
in residuary stasis while what changes, changes.

It's like the lake itself, the water held
for a geologic second in banks left behind
as residual debris by the last passing glacier.

The lake reclines in her bed. Wet glacial residue.
The lake knows that she stays for only a little while,
part of her always seeping out or evaporating,

part of her replenished by rain, by the lakes
above her in a chain of glacial kettles, part by springs
swollen through between-drought generosity.

The lake knows that someday she will either dry up
or will overflow her banks somewhere and rejoin the flow
she has been only a stopover for these few flowing millennia.

But the lake doesn't care, doesn't need to care.
In whatever shape, in whatever place or places,
or whatever momentum, the lake is what she is.

Residuary here, then, we take our dimensions
from the lake herself, our part of her space, our fate
to take part in *her* sense of time, and not our own.

Selenity Book Four

Glare

Waves slip and clip by us
in a tempo of tipsy marimbas.
The breeze picks up,
thirsting for waves.
Waves slurp at the sky.

Waves slap, a madness—
the insane flapping
of thick loons in thin air—
like mine, the wrong element.

The waves peck and slurp
at surface prey, which
has all died out this late
in an exhausted leaf-fall.
Prey cowers below the waves.

A surge below drives waves
sky-ward—toward the lake-
devouring haze of sun.
Below, fish devour each other.

Waves troll our still boat
northwards, toward
the chill glimmer and weave
of ultimate borealis, the rare
visible music of night.

Loonshine

After all, it is the nature of loons to swim
even under boats sometimes
but not under this one before, not ours,
not until now

nor wearing these clusters of silver
pearls on her back, which shine, gleam,
pure glow! beneath the lake surface:
The silver of it!

The emerald of its dive.
And not a glisten of it for me alone.
This elemental lack is oxygen
to my moment of joy.

What did Francis declare to be perfect joy?
My joy, likewise severe and likewise difficult
and likewise nowise cursed by perfection,
follows the deepening shine of the bird.

Cold and Bright, the View from Below

It is desert, the depths
of this cold lake
where its wealth of scarcity
invites few as residents,
only survivors
or the drowned.

Still though, undrowned
we can imagine the apposite sky
above where we are only
pretending to breathe
in pre-pneumonic silence.

We can stare from below
the rippling surface
of the bluebright daylight
as through a bottle-bottom
shard of ancient windowglass

from the undersurface out
to the blue rose of receding day
perfectly clear
in the sanctified crackle
to read the illuminated
pages of the distant sun.

Fall Harvest

My dock will be out until the first sowing of winter.
Then Ben and the boys will bring it to shore, a harvest,
section by section. Free the shore to ancient time.

Then the lake will be open to winter, shore empty
of human traffic. We will see deer drinking on shore
and now and then a stag with his randy rack of antlers.

The leaves will have fallen, save for those of a few
recalcitrant oaks, always the last to loose their grip
of labor. The forest will have opened for winter.

Long-dead aspen will show again, lying as always,
their heads, shorn of rotted tree-tops, all facing sunrise.
I will turn and face the sunset. Sunset is the drive back

to the desert where we face the subtler and sadder
fall, a slight twinge of cool *déjà vu* to mark the season.
Closer each fall, in joy I face sunset, toward harvest.

Notes in Black and White

In a black and white photo,
the canine clarity,
the absence
of color dominates
the scene in such
a way that the scene
disappears
in favor of its particulars

as color becomes dispensable
and the scene belongs
to the mind striving
to fare far out
from the prescribed
bounds of eyesight.
    *

Rafting white water
you see best
through the cold white
splash on your face.
    *

To look into the lake
on a day of such clarity of depth,
but no visible bottom
by which we can test
the intrusions of reality,

to see so far into the water
is to see into collodion
emulsions of clear
oblivion,
a perfect obsidian
refracted out of sunlight.

Badlands

It is because the lake is so clear this summer.
The bottom disappears.
Disappears?
A cloud bank covers the only blue left for a while.

Then just under the deception of glitter,
surface ripples like knapped sky, flint-deep.
The lake deepens to dark charcoal.
Ancient lava flowing under the surface.

Still and hard below.
Malpais.
The disparate translucencies of lake a mile above the pillow
of set lava balanced precarious above the igneous flow

that stood still for the creation of the first
minuscule death—the comedy
that dies still after aeons of learning.
A Folsom point. Obsidian lens.

Lucretius' Dervish

Once I could enjoy
      sitting for what
           seemed to be
      listless and perfect
hours watching Sufi
      motes dance among
           listless bars of
      sunlight flowing
from my window.
      Now I do not think
           I can see
      those motes any
longer, though sunlight
      bars still attract
           the microscopic
      to my inner eyes. Nor
do I float or spin
      in dreams any longer.
           Except for now,
      when sun-charged
motes twirl again,
      and my meandering
           pencil distracts
      my eyes from needing
to see.

August Afternoon at Play

Dozers and graders have dug and straightened
and smoothed a new six-foot berm in the landfill.
We back the pickup near the berm—the new spot

for new trash—remove our ladder and haul the load
of cut palo verde and mesquite out by the thick ends
of the branches, lay it down all of a thorny piece.

A dump-truck pulls up, noses up to the high berm,
drops a load of busted-up road—concrete chunks,
hundreds of pounds per chunk—behind the truck.

Berm at the nose end, concrete at the ass end,
he scratches his pate and asks if we have a shovel.
We wonder to him what good it would do

if we *did* have a shovel. He climbs into the cab and sits.
We listen to the news for a few minutes and smoke.
Then we leave, and we leave our ladder behind us.

"We work together . . ." thinking ahead or not.
In the desert summer, heat is the equalizer,
maker of the common mind, our *genius ludi*.

"It Might Be Nice if We Brought Flowers"
for Sophia

Can it be true about any life in any species
that the only good one is a dead one?
The "nice" scorpion from the terrarium, as you say,

though dead by all reports, has not become nice
by virtue of death but by the nature of its relation
in re:

its un-lonely surviving partner in their glassed-in world.
The nice scorpion who-has-been survives just enough to continue
as recorded *nice* in the primordial milieu of arthropod un-niceness.

But these comparisons dissolve with your expression of grief.
"It might be nice if we brought flowers." Even slyly,
you care to regard the departed in your gentle mind

an impulse toward fragile memorial beauty
in deference to a perceived Ordovician decorum
offered this lonely survivor,

who, a scorpion after all, has never been lonely
in its non-company with its once-and-ever nice companion,
nor now, in company no more or less tender or

nice than any company, save what your young soul endows,
than it had enjoyed by way of its primordial nature,
never noticed before your blossoming moment of grace.

Elegy for the Last Iguanodon
in Memory of Intwy

O Great Cud!
Magnificant Chomper!
You have not chewed on
Earth these epochs past.
Thousands of millennia, all lorn now
since we have chanced to converse
at the distance of time and size
your dinosaurian
eminence commands,

behind eyelids pressed
hard to my pre-memory
I see you wrest dumptrucks of milfoil
and swamp iris
from the muck at the lake shore—
your beak, so massive, so delicate.
I watch you chomp the green stems and leaves'
purple and blue spring and summer blossoms—
loosestrife, heal-all, pickerelweed, gentian.
And green—amaranth
and asphodel of Elysian pasture.

Back and forth slide
your hugely engineered jaws
so finely evolved out of the dim
birdiness of your ancestors—
back and forth in contemplative slowness
while the shadows of
the shadows of poems
undulate in the skull that sweeps slowly
back and forth, back and forth
over the disintegrating gallons of undressed salad.

> > >

Selenity Book Four

I would sing the blues for you but your world
is so green, so moist—soft green slowly
blackening into the slurry of progress—
that I cannot refract
from the sheen the blues I feel.
So I will sing the greens for you
a trope of green counterpoint to the dirge
that mourns your innocent extinction.
Chew on, chew on, carbonic emblem
of our disposable human future.
Chew on, Iguanodon.
Chew on.

Overcast

Upsittingly I Am Arranged

Upsittingly I am arranged in this wooden desk chair, borrowed.
I have engineered and organized myself into a perfect discomfort,
        a plinth of virtue.

I invite my sheltered soul to open the fine expanse of window.
Six implacable panes, each about three by six feet.

Each a vertical grave.
A treacherous transparency of clear glass wall.
Each should be opaque for all the world they let in for us to touch.

Come. Stare at the view with me.
Admire the two small trees, acacias of some sort, or wattle,
        leather leaves of thrifty desert evolution.

I have time on my hands and my numbing backside
        to wonder what the trees—

as foreign as we are here, as the windows are,
        as the air in our breathless new world, the all-indoors—
    what the trees, that is, might call themselves.

On the other side of the tarmac drive a wall protects the drive and us
        from the threatening purity of green in the park we cannot see.
I am protected, as you are while you maybe only visit.

In the farthest distance a pale healthfulness of eucalyptus.
Just beyond the wall, sixteen strata of six-inch concrete blocks,
        two large leafless trees, probably pecans.

It is March.
Whatever season or topology it is in here where we are so protected,
        it is desert out there, irrigated to conform to the temperate
        world of pecans.

                                                                      > > >

If you and I could see through the wall!
We'd see the pecans waiting to bud.
Should not have long to wait.

I sit in the hardwood chair in the air conditioning.
Were I a child again I could pretend again.
I could pretend that the bare pecan trees are waiting for me to climb
and shake them into green.

But I am a civilized victim of maturity.
I sit anciently on the wooden desk chair in the air conditioning
       behind the impenetrable glass.
The trees cannot hear me or you through the mechanical integrity.

We can no longer begin or pretend to hear the trees.
We can no longer reach the first branch to begin again.
The good ache in the infinity of our child's upward scramble maybe
       way up that eucalyptus in the farthest clearest distance.

Do you remember the clarity?
High enough and in such danger of height and invention.
When we embraced the tree for our only protection the tree
       whispered back its name.

Unremembering
       we listened.

Cell Phone

Exhaustible patience.
Pristine clarity of our meditations
shattered into a clatter of rude molecules

from someone else's rainbow, unreachable
save by more than ordinary eyes,
all broken and only because a pair of pants

has burst into song.

"*La Plume de*"... The Candy Wrappers of History

"God!" the second-year student whines,
"They claim to love the environment,
but they don't even recycle!"

In his third year he may take
Foundations of Western Philosophy
and contemplate the nature of his pique,

welcome himself, in *Themes of Western History*,
to Sixteenth Century London, Twelfth Century Rome,
First Century Jerusalem.

But if he fails to recycle the scraps—as he will—
the printed pages, the vellum palimpsests,
the speculative papyri of these stories,

he might as well toss that Snickers wrapper he's holding
right there on the mall on his way to his midterm exam
in *Intro to Ecology* and his un-memorable blue book.

To do the right thing right, it is sensible first to wonder why.

A Capitalist

Why did the boat-tail
grackle do that,

tong his beak around
a three-quarter inch cube

of Potatoes O'Brien?
Unless he wanted

to prove to himself
that he could do it,

and that the next
grackle could not,

and would not get
the chance anyway

because the first
grackle had filled

its craw for the sake
of the indigestible.

Feeding

A Gila woodpecker
approaches the peaceful station
of our vulnerable hummingbird feeder.
The woodpecker attacks, or seems to,
has no choice not to, no matter how peaceful
the bird is in his neighborly intentions.

Lacking the hummingbird's instinct and skill
for control in stasis,
lacking a perch to sip politely from,
the clumsy woodpecker
catches such of our imitation nectar as it catches
by ramming itself against the plastic flower—

a battleship trying to nudge its way
alongside a poor fisherman's wooden pier,
in just the careless manic discourtesy
by which the creatures who manufacture
imitation nectar and plastic blossoms
drive away the hummingbirds of nations—

the brute innocence of unexamined power.

Patriot Two-Step

Elevated like saints we trip
lightly above blighted Earth.

The soles of our inflated
jogging shoes are clean.

But the soul of our collective
blemish of mind treads heavily

among dogmas, creeds, strip mines,
nuclear desire and death wish—

children's bones in mine fields,
and our many armies' detritus of flags.

A Grace from the Usurer
in dubious honor of Robert Rector and the Heritage Foundation

"They can't be poor.
They have refrigerators.
Let them afford their refrigerators.
Let them afford
the gift of the refrigerators we sell them.
Let them afford
some of the cost of the food
in the refrigerators we may repossess.

"Let them,
if they can and Oh . . .
Oh we think they can, know they will,
should agree to, pay interest on
credit cards for the food they lavish
on their refrigerators,
pay for the copper they borrow with the gold
we demand.

"So that
they will have nothing left
whereby
to afford the painful luxury of their tears:
Wherefore
we do declare them happy.
And so shall they be.
And we shall be consoled."

Selenity Book Four

Life and Dis-Life in the Late Anthropocene

We try to share so much as we can of what we hope
    might be the animals' freedom,
        what's left of it behind the barriers,
    pacing ruts round and round the airy cages
behind the bars, the plexiglass,
    the clever moats: the lies,
        the optical lies that lie before and behind bars,
    or on either side of moats,
the silent lies of imitation horizon.

We share such little as we can of the anger we anticipate we would feel,
    trapped as we are on the other side,
        pacing for food, hiding nowhere—

We've been walking through the zoo now for many years, almost fifty.
    Same zoo.
        Used to take the kids to the zoo.
            Watch the animals.
Picnics.
    Kids loved the zoo.
        We all did. We all did.

But I can't say we have ever been to the zoo without feeling this vague
    guilt for the killing that made a zoo the only world
        left for the animals,
    the choking gall of irony behind it,
and the anger.
But whose anger?
    Ours partly.
        Animals' maybe.

We duck our heads and run for the inner comfort and gloom
    of our fabricated lair, and the conscience we consume
        when we visit the zoo.

> > >

Our kids all grown, we still pretend for them, alone.

Only the flying creatures,
> descendants of the fourth freedom of evolution,
>> are free here at the zoo.

The lesser among us, we will not fly.

Selenity Book Four

Time Scale

In a new development in this desert,
all life—cactus, ocotillo, mesquite, creosote-bush,
cinnabar tinted quartz—*all life*

draglined and backhoed
into another new suburban diaspora—
scorpions waited.

After the block walls had risen
and the unguarded moon had risen,
the scorpions began to climb up out of their eons

like the time-line in your old geology book.
The scorpions took the vertical way
out of the Ordovician to the site of your mortgage.

Then the pest-control trucks appeared
and poison-hoses blasted the scorpions back,
but not to the oblivion you wanted them.

Scorpion tracks,
when you look into your conscience, mark
the rock-wall punctuation between dream-house and dream.

Scorpions climb up over the night-wall of your waking,
skitter unheard into the interstices of your impervious
rattling scales.

Eumaeus Old Tends to Conveniences

An accident out there on 41st Street, Sioux Falls.
And after we returned to the Best Western
after we had grabbed a meal at Olive Garden,
where the Zuppa Toscana is to be recommended
way above the Chicken Marsala, in Sioux Falls,

after, anyway, we returned to our room (do
you know what it's like not to remember
your room number if you are an old person
in the era of the un-numbered Key Card?)
which, lucky for us, is placed in an obvious corner—

and after I had returned to my MacBook Air
to test the air for information on The Orphans' Train
that I wanted for a more difficult poem than this
promises to be, and after it wouldn't connect and after
Carol had tried the TV to check out HBO which

we refuse to have at home anyway, in preference
to more æsthetic efforts, like . . . well, like what?
That is when she let me know that we had no TV
in the room. So, for the first time ever, I read
through today's *USA Today*. Blackout all around.

Selenity Book Four

Waiting for the Tweet of Doom

The Day of Judgment dawned
on, let us say, a late spring morn
in Eighteen Forty-Three @2:28 a.m.

The issue is not to be argued.
The information may be Googled.
Then the information Googlee

may become the information
Googler and Google me.
Then we will both know.

Then the info-Googler will Tweet
to her/his Tweetees and the Tweetees
will Tweet to the World,

and the World will know. Tweeters
will buzz (for if a Tweeter can buzz,
what can a Tweeter not do?)

and Truth will flow like amber.
April 27, to be precise, @2:28 a.m.
in Eighteen Forty-Three.

Break: Setting at Day-Break

Soliloquy by the Candle Light of Day
for Caedmon

I wake up again to clouds—
clouds, dull linens of clouds
to lines, words of poems
soft dull linens of words

on the fore and plowing edge of a determined
raft of dream surging down some sleep-powered wake.
I knew I could wake up—get up
fumble for one of the pencils on my bedside table

and one of the folded shirt-pocket size
discarded memories of scarified paper
write the words or the lines or
once or twice

lines of music whose delicacies I cannot notate
nor ever learned how.
But I knew alerted by the clear spray of ideas now
that I would remember in the morning.

I never did. Did you? Ever?
But one night I dreamt some of those words again
or lines or prisms of image in the foam of notes.
Then I dreamt that I got up

got out of bed
picked up a pencil
found a folded paper
and then I dreamt that I wrote it all down.

All and beautiful—and all in a murky second gone into the foam.
I've never dreamt such dream again
but some urge behind the surge of dream told me
to write for the fabric of dream, the linen shadows of clouds   > > >

anything at all, anything away from my sullen old silence.
Though it is a grace of old age the dream has been good,
a faith in dreams of embers all these lights ago—the
"highest candle lights in the dark,"

which dark
needs no more than a candle
and less
to read into the wakening heaves of breath in a new old life.

Part Two: What We Learn, What We Become
For and in memory of Nick Salerno, Magister et Frater

This is our wedding picture. That is, it was taken at my wedding with Carol, whom I have lived with and loved for over fifty years. Nick was my best man, and Nick remained my best man until he died last spring. I am no Prospero, nor do I give up this third of my life willingly; I resign myself with the notion that, one third now gone into memory, two thirds of my life remain, one third in thoughtful diminishment.

I had not thought much about doing another book. Nothing against a new book, I just hadn't thought about it. After Nick died, though, I took stock, as one will do when he loses a third of his life. Among the stock, near neither the top nor the bottom nor maybe the middle was a cache of many more published poems than I had realized. Much of the book is viewed from below, but that is to be regarded, I hope, as uplifting—any direction one takes being a direction. And taken. Besides, the water is clear.

For the Living . . . and the Living
Kathy Harris, friend and guide for fifty years

Kathryn Harris 1941-2015

I move from rotting branch to rotting branch
under my feet in a boggy forest
but I will not get lost while the thrush sings.

I will move from black branch to black branch
in the sun defying forest
an anthracite sheen of lively decay.

And I cannot become lost, not
into this glow from the lure of darkness visible.
But what if the thrush does stop singing?

From *Eumaeus Tends,* of which Kathy approved.
It's been a year now. Thrush sings.

Working Verse around the Green Commons
for Paul Mariani

We walked the pasture and ancient tillage of field from party to dinner
at the old inn, at whose door we were separated into our ordinary offices.

Your lines are too short you said shortly as I stopped talking
for a nervous breath both of us avoiding contention and the discomfort

that so often precedes the finality of understanding and maybe
the decision that orients the level of friendship or mere acquaintance.

Your lines
are too long
I replied.

The short line
may be a sigh
or a gasp for
the comings
and goings of
inter

rupted breathing

the staccato comings and goings and lornful longings of inter

rupted living

                                                                        > > >

that serve to disguise the wordless interstices in which we try
actually to exist and hold our breath before the inter

ruption
of a catastasis
like the chosen word
leading toward
mutual enlightenment.

Enlightened,
we have not spoken for thirty years
though I have noticed over those years

that our lines
have tended toward compromise
mostly in the direction of *your* line length.

Thus we have shared an appropriate communication
between incompatible spiritualities, turning
among the verses toward a shared communal tillage.

Selenity Book Four

Words with Heraclitus

1
They say that the sun has been
865,000 miles wide

almost all the long eons since its birth.
To Heraclitus the sun is one foot wide.

In another two and a half millennia
will the sun be that much narrower

by geometric measure and moral erosion
or humans that much greater?

Will humans then be able to see
the sun as it is, or themselves as they are?

2
Be all that you are or can be!
Be rich!

How can any fate be direr?
Unless you also long for power.

3
In his moment of errant confidence
Heraclitus declaims

Now that we can travel anywhere,
we need no longer take the poets

and myth-makers for sure witnesses
about disputed facts.*

Traveling out for the morning sun
Eumaeus scratches his dinner behind the ear

and does not say aloud:

*Now that we know that however far
we travel we are in the vastness:*

*nowhere yet,
how can we hope to arrive without*

*poets and myth-makers for mused
witness among disputed facts?*

4
Heraclitus:

*The soul is undiscovered
though explored forever
to a depth beyond report—**

5
Eumaeus:

*[while the poet's words
explore breath by breath to
report beyond depth.]*

Once he'd got there, Heraclitus
claimed that you can't get there
from here—you.

But that's neither here
nor there

> > >

Selenity Book Four

*since we're almost always
either in one place
or another*

*always in one time
or another*

*or always all ways
and any where.*

**Heraclitus: Fragments*, translated by Brooks Haxton.

The Newly Risen

Her scattered gear lived
the free life under the aqueduct:
auto aqueduct: freeway.

Concrete shadows create for blindered drivers
a cathedral arch beneath the underpass,
new underpass then, in eager dayglo gray,

bright with sun north and south,
bright with new concrete.
Bright with a public joy of freedom:

bright with fresh shrubbery under the carven concrete
cathedral tracery through which angels imagine themselves
into existence and flight.

New Jerusalem Wonder
(in the slums of a county island),
angels above nave and transom, and . . . ah . . .

Bright gold. Golden daylight.
Silver moon.
Silver sheen in the cool of her nights.

She, who was the sole and soul-priestess
of all this, priestess of the appropriated shopping cart,
whose vision was all this bright temple,

looked into the gentle eyes of our forgiving community,
raised her supplicating arms heaven-ward,
accepting its *warm breast and ah! bright wings. And flew!*

No. We see what we need to see, seldom seeing.
Look again when you are stopped for that light.
Take your eyes from the angry face of the next driver.   > > >

Selenity Book Four

See only:

a pile of your gray detritus abandoned
under a pile of your gray detritus
under our shared detritus of what once was sky.

She is buried now, surely you fail to acknowledge,
under what was
sky.

A Child

. . . and I think of her
not only for the minutes
I hold her in the writing

but for the soul of her
that lives in the writing,
only in the writing
because of those minutes.

All that we love should
be held, not believed in,
but held close. And gently.

And believed in.

Selenity Book Four

"O Crustacean"
(a greeting from Ed Wade to Uncle crust)

Chitinous cousin to our hemichordate memories
remind us of our intimate
cellular closeness to every other cell,

our own pasts rendered into fibrous hues of keratin,
our hostile distance carefully composed in
anodyne gesture-armored courtesy.

Scales. Horn. Pre-cancerous
connection to the first
aggressive cellular mutation.

It is time we were made aware of our state
in the great microbial condition.
It is time we are formally introduced.

O, of course.

Richard, I'd like to introduce
you to Mammalian Evolution. You two
have much in common. Very much.

Pleased to meetcha.

Old Dogs from ancienter pasts.
Opabinia, far-and-near sighted.
Dvinia, small, Earth-sheltered.
A new trick every epoch or so.

Tricks for the next Big Event.
Opposable thumb, binocular vision.
Then the same old Extinction again.

Life roars.
Earth yawns.
Gapes.

Silence of Echoes in Caves
Notes in Extension of a Story I Don't Remember
Owing to the Distraction of Extending

Demodocus old, older.
Desiccated below him the Holy Vale.
He sits atop the hill or mound or mountain of his mind.

He thinks and he tries to remember
and as he remembers his heels dig
their stolid dance into the soft dust of clay.

Heels search for a rock in the clay that will brace his feet,
tune the dance, stiffen a rhythm of his back and his spirit
for the renewal of upward heave,

Hephaestian ulcerous belch,
fiery healing
draws from below the heavy cairns of his pasts and his futures.

The top of this wind-slick carapace of Terrapin Earth
resides above that accident of erosion,
the cave carved by seasons of extinct spring flood

and internal maelstrom
and the windings of the roots of a great olive whose ancient story
shades the old poet in his silent cloud-borne mourning.

The agon between a meandering wan spirit and the unmovable change below—
the cave, the dug tomb, the undertomb of anxiety,
the rising fire.

The silence of echo is a sound of caves that we may stand above,
pray into with healing despair of breath, effort, faith.
None or all.

> > >

Selenity Book Four

Fraying shadows fail like web in a fantasy of care,
part nightmare,
binds loneliness to a heavy distance of the body,

feet struggling against the soft clay that shivers from beneath our feet—
the slice and slide of line between ourselves and the weight of nothing
save the root-bound tomb.

To let go now drops nothing.
The old poet opens words again to the ghosts of Ithaca lost,
and will not let go.

Demodocus breathes shadows in my direction.
The same small voice: *Richard. Here.*
The ashes of Ithaca, of Tempe, the breath shivers, *to blend with your own.*

Your hand?

The Little Bang:
a Poem-Cartoon about Drought from 2 Lines of John Ashbery
"Only a 28 year water supply
shields us from the . . ."
"Floating Away," from *Planisphere*

Part 1: Rain

Twenty-seven
        Twenty-six
                Twenty-five
        Twenty-four
Twenty-three
        Twenty-two
                Twenty-one
        Twenty
Nineteen

2: The Wreckage of the Sky

Eighteen
        Seventeen
                Sixteen
        Fifteen
Fourteen
        Thirteen
                Twelve
        Eleven
Ten

Part 3: Uncle Deity

Nine
        Eight
                Seven   > > >

Selenity Book Four

	Six	
Five		
	Four	
		Three
	Two	
One		

Part 4: The Holy Man in the Final Shade

. . . desert."
       o
              -1
      Pfffff . . .
fffft:

       pop!

            [bang!]

The Older

The older you get
the more sounds you hear in the night, and louder.

The older you get
the older the sounds in the night, the abyssal echo.

The older you get
the more the sounds in the night echo a memory

of places you've never been,
of places that *have* never been.

The older you get
the more those places resemble

the Nothing you try to imagine
and the more you try to imagine

the more you approach all that there is,
the more you become all that there is.

The more you become all that there is,
the Nothing that is cannot go away.

The older you get
the more you become.

And Nothing.

Selenity Book Four

A State of Poise

Does exist an attitude, a turn of the head
poised better to see, hear, and respond?
A special position of lens?

Does exist a level of doubt
that should rise beyond doubt, but retain
doubt as well in a maze of questions?

Ours has become a world that fires beliefs like bullets,
shoots out at non-belief, at any question—
strafes the precious Other

and burns, devours, engorges on others' healing doubt
at the common altar of backyard
barbecue, the sixpack-scripture-world

that refuses to hear the word "question."
Somewhere in the barrage of narrative
will we sometime discover Narrative?

And will the narrative be written
in words that are not curses?
In gestures unaccompanied by deadly projectiles?

The Becoming

The lake bottom we drift over
is unremarkable, like,
well, any other lake bottom.

Sand.
A carpet of bushy low water plants.
White shells of defunct tiny clams.

Rocks
encrusted in whatever it is
that encrusts rocks in lake water.

The few thousands of years
that this bottom has been visible
as rocks grow more encrusted in . . . rock leather?

Color is for the ancient oceans
painted in eons of contending life.
Here in the lake, life

is as transient as lakes are to geology,
ephemera of scant time in evolution,
dying in millennia that are seconds to eons.

Let that bare equation serve to mark the potential beauty
down there under the clarity, waiting as we wait
to become part of the dying landscape.

Selenity Book Four

Codex, A Case for the Lonely Poet

Codex, A Case for the Lonely Poet

First one. First try fail better one. Something there badly not wrong. Not that as it is it is not bad. The noface bad. The no hands bad. The no—. Enough. A pox on bad. Mere bad. Way for worse.[i]

If what follows maintains a course it will do so mostly without me. So it may be confusing. I hope so. If what follows makes sense, then I have done the job wrong. If it leads you toward discovering something like sense on your own, then I have succeeded. Too well, I suspect. A starting point somewhere between the two poles will satisfy me. So will anywhere around the poles. Anywhere, but Somewhere. Indeed, I hope that it remains confusing to all of us, because I want to say something about independence among poets, but I want to do it by way of my own stumbling adventure with a poem, whether I am writing it or reading it. And that is confusing. I will add here that I will seem to leave out everyone in the writing world but poets. I would apologize, but I don't write novels, nor "creative nonfiction" nor . . . you understand. Besides, poets were here first, and no writer worth the language is entitled to abandon Genesis. AND: all literature that is literature is made up of poetry.

*

If you ask me why I write "something like poetry"[ii] I might shuffle about, grin innocently and joke that I like to communicate with the people who knew Homer and visited with Odysseus at home. It can't possibly be true.

It is true.

Engaging in poetry as poet—as reader, as LISTENER, as tolerated if not welcome participant—is engaging with the late simian re-vision of the very beginning, the world before poetry, the world before words. And that return destroys utterly the future of poetry. Only it doesn't; it can't. It does eliminate the possibility of poetry, of any art, even as a profession.

But of course and again, it doesn't. Art, like Walt, is large, a kosmos, and contains multitudes, including professional artists.

*

A. R. Ammons, who spent most of his life teaching poetry, which means classes and workshops, was nevertheless always an outsider, never sure about his status as a professor or poet paddling around the mainstream. He tried not to take it personally. What he said about government support of the arts is, in part:

> I detest the averaging down of expectation and dedication that occurs when thousands of poets are given money in what is really waste and welfare, not art at all ... The genuine is lost, and the whole field wallops with political and social distortions.[iii]

Ammons fails to provide alternative suggestions for independent poets. The independent poet already knows what to do: be independent—and stay in the world he needs to stay in. The day job. Also, very likely, the night job. That the job might be teaching, even teaching writing in a college, doesn't matter so much as experience in a world matters: the C. W. workshop, a whaling ship, a bedroom and garden in Amherst, a desk in an office in Hartford, working in a pool hall and tutoring, teaching third grade. What works. [iv]

*

When I look in the backs of anthologies at the biographies of poets these days, I am not surprised that almost all of the contributors are products of MFA programs and that they are most likely to teach creative writing at colleges and universities. That this system is responsible for a stolid quality of inbreeding and secular ecclesiastics with acolytes training acolytes is not the point of this essay.

Still:

Mark Edmundson, whose own notion of poetry I think to be a touch sonorous by today's standards, nevertheless makes a potent case against our reliance on the institution of the MFA workshop degree.

> To thrive in this process you often must write in the mode of the

mentor—you must play the game that is there to be played. You must be a member of the school, you must sing in the correct key. If you try to overwhelm the sponsor, explode his work into irrelevance— well, the first law of success is simple: Never outshine the master . . . The master will not like it—and there will be no first book, no fellowship, no job, no preferment. It is only by making the master look more accomplished, by writing in his mode, becoming a disciple, that the novice ascends . . .

To thrive in the world of contemporary poetry, to thrive at court, you had best play it safe, offend none.[v]

Although the comments are reminiscent of Dr. Johnson's complaints about patronage (which he grudgingly accepted anyway), Edmondson's view is harsh. Certainly he knows that the artist will take what she needs from the program she has entered with both optimism and skepticism, and she will, as she learns to learn for herself, take what works and leave what doesn't. She may save her overt displays of independence (rebellion and revelation) for her real world, and she may even discover what real worlds exist for her.

Or not. Or not. Or not.

*

The artistic life I want to contemplate is the ancient, sacred and disregarded primordium that poets still come from, the old array of human characters who have been driven to look at the world, and beyond the world, in ways that may be accompanied by the lyre. Most of us these days seem to have been bred by the fires of MFA programs, like salamanders, but some of us also know that our fires are confined neither to institutions nor myth. We are what we come from.

Like for instance:

I don't know how many poets have spent their careers teaching at the elementary and high school levels. Not many, I think, not so much because these poets don't exist as that they have no institution to support them. So I will try to speak for my anonymous colleagues when I declare that we are the appropriate subject and audience for

Tomas Tranströmer's poem, "Codex." We represent the anonymous practitioners who spend their lives quietly transforming and transferring the culture to next and next and next generations, in a strong sense all at once, those minds who eventually and somehow joyfully

> . . . can no longer receive
> have not stopped giving.
> They rolled out a little of the radiant and melancholy tapestry
> and let go again.
> They are anonymous, they are my friends
> without my knowing them . . .

They are like members of my own ancestral family, names mostly never known, or forgotten, or moiled into the vaguest generic mythos of unheeded family tales; men and women—mostly women—who, whatever their official life-calling might have been, somehow managed to spend much of their lives in the front of the classroom, adding words to the "Codex."

It's an attempt to take nothing as ever finished, but so far as we can, always to translate, transform, transfer, "to step over the border without anyone noticing . . ."

*

In European caves, among what are now fragile treasures of what we see as art, besides the pictures of great animals—bison, rhinoceros, aurochs, lion—are handprints. Handprints, among the rarity of the caves, are not uncommon. But in Chauvet Cave[vi] the little finger of the limned hand is slightly bent. We cannot assume that the hand was chosen on behalf of this trivial misfeature. It is, we assume, a hand communicating—what? It is not our language; we have no language for what we see; we cannot see without language. For us, it is only the bent finger that suggests language—a signature; we cannot help but interpret. It is no more than a flaw, a repeated visual hiccup. If it were speech—poetry—we might hear it, see it, as a stammer, an interruption to the flow of sense that would stop us—and we are stopped—to consider what, in the flow of the poem suddenly sends us beyond language.

*

Sometime during my first years of graduate school I bought the brand new volume *Poetry: The Golden Anniversary Issue*.[vii] I still have it. It's right over there on the fourth shelf up, to the right, a little more, that's it. I know, it's pretty small, but that's all the bigger it needs to be.

Actually, because I am writing several hundred miles from that book shelf, I am not really looking at the book. I don't really need to. Neither do you. If you know who was writing poetry between 1912 and 1968, just in general—this isn't a test—then you know who are represented in this little volume. You may not like all of their work; in fact, you may react almost violently to some of the most famous of it, but you can't really get away from it, whether you want to or not. And you do want to, and you do not want to.

I used to subscribe to *Poetry*. I haven't for over a decade. One of my friends still subscribes, but he admits that the reasons fall between hope for improvement and a stubborn defeatism. But I have gotten mail from *Poetry*.

Here is part of one such letter, one that I have received at least twice in the last few years:

> Dear Reader:
>   It is difficult
> to get the news from poems
>   yet men die miserably every day
>   for lack
> of what is found there.
>
>   —from Asphodel, "That Greeny Flower"
>
> When William Carlos Williams wrote the lines above, he didn't mean them literally—as if a poem a day, like an apple, would keep the doctor away. What he meant was that poetry nourishes us, and refreshes and helps us discover the meaning of our daily existence.

I do not know that I can argue with that, so far as it takes me. But it doesn't take me farther than so many other matters that refresh me and help me discover the meaning of my daily existence: my morning coffee, a cool shower on a hot day, rain drops on roses, whiskers on kittens, crisp apple strudel[viii] and even many not so favorite things.

William Carlos Williams cannot have been so dull-witted the

day he wrote those lines! "Men die miserably every day for lack of what is found there"! The sentiment is uplifting, no doubt, but the image is horrifying. He is referring to what may be found in what he calls, just above these lines, "despised poems." If the banner representative of America's premier (and wealthiest) poetry magazine can fail to read what is on the page, what purpose can the magazine really have these days than—like any successful institution, universities for instance—to perpetuate itself? Surely, something there is in poetry that is more than mere *Poetry*, or why does some of it stick around so long?

> To foe of His—I'm deadly foe—
> None stir the second time—
> On whom I lay a Yellow Eye—
> Or an emphatic thumb—
>
> Though I than He—may longer live
> He longer must—than I—
> For I have but the power to kill,
> Without—the power to die—   764[ix]

Or, re-translating the brief entirety, much has been made of:

> Eros makes me shiver again
> Strengthless in the knees
> Eros gall and honey,
> Snake-sly, invincible.[x]

More nearly literal:

> Eros the melter of limbs (now again) stirs me
> sweetbitter unmaneagable creature who steals in

Or, how much poetry can be made, on either side of the brackets (which indicate missing pieces):

> and this   [
> ruinous god   [
>
> I swear did not love   [
> but now because   [

Selenity Book Four

>   and the reason neither   [
>   nothing much   [[xi]

Early translators, frustrated at the fragmentary beauty of Sappho's poetry, compelled themselves to "translate" into what couldn't have been Sappho. What can be translated from Sappho into the New?

*

John Barr served as the first president of the Poetry Foundation (whence, these days, *Poetry* magazine). In September 1996 *Poetry* published Barr's essay "American Poetry in the New Century." Among his comments he declared, "American poetry is ready for something new because our poets have been writing in the same way for a long time now. There is fatigue, something stagnant about the poetry written today." The letter from the magazine that I quote from above came to me the last time in 2014. The more things change . . .

Whatever the goal of any institution—a church, a university, a government, a corporation, a poetry foundation—as it succeeds, it fails. Its purpose evolves to avoid failure, or the fear of failure, by resorting to schemes of self-preservation, benign or ruthless—both usually. As our purpose as artists, whatever we think the purpose is, is partly not to fail, we can do no more than to take what the institution offers and then grow without it. Or, grow without it from the start. But grow.

*

The finger continues to beckon. Some caves are still, to geologists, alive. To the artist, in caves like Chauvet, images still stop us for want of words, including ours. The images and we stand by helplessly stammering and staggeringly unapproachable, and staggeringly alive. Here is a stammer; a mystery of stammers—of hesitation—of nearly unspoken—unspeakable perhaps—Threats ("A sumptuous Destitution") to all that we Think we Perceive:

> In many and reportless places
> We feel a Joy—
> Reportless, also, but sincere as Nature
> Or Deity—

> It comes, without a consternation—
> Dissolves—the same—
> But leaves a sumptuous Destitution—
> Without a Name—
>
> Profane it by a search—we cannot
> It has no home—
> Nor we who having once inhaled it—
> Therefore roam.[xii] (1382)

To where did Emily Dickinson roam? Only into and through the poem and into Eternity in order to battle the Inventor of Eternity—to the Death. I don't think that Dickinson is being coy in the feeling of line 2; I do think that she aims toward a joy that is unique in its defiance of what we are taught by culture to think of as "Joy." It is a terrible Joy that is born of a poet's freedom and aloneness:

> On this heath wrecked from Genesis, nerve endings quicken. Naked sensibility at the extremest periphery. Narrative expanding contracting dissolving. Nearer to know less before afterward schism in sum. No hierarchy, no motion of polarity.[xiii]

Workshops do not need to teach such language. Can they, in fact? What Dickinson learned of life through her poetry could not have been learned from life in Amherst alone, either through cooperation with her own culture or kneeling at the feet of her distant "Master." What Howe learns from Dickinson, and what she learns from her own writing (prosepoetry?) about Dickinson's writing does not come from classroom or workshop.

*

A. R. Ammons seems, at least in part, to have enjoyed the inspiration for *Sphere: The Form of a Motion* from a faculty meeting: listening: listening? being there? playing with his car keys while his attention was directed toward the door? Or the notion he may have played with in his mind in or out of the pulse of a meeting: The One and the Many probably: when someone suggested that some notion be put in "the form of a motion." O, yeah. What is more formless than motion: what is more formed that the effort of following the motion? (The colon was Ammons' trademark punctuation.)

Selenity Book Four

the shapes nearest shapelessness awe us most, suggest
the god: elemental air in a spin, counterclockwise
for us, lets its needlepoint funnel down and gives us

a rugged variety of the formless formed:[xiv]

*

"We approach the task of listening / Through the veil of meaningless distraction."[xv]

*

I looked back at the very beginning of this just to see if I had come to a reasonable conclusion to the troubles, or if I were still confused. I am proud to assert that my intention that the piece would maintain its course without me, and that I would remain confused, has come to pass. On the other hand, I have to admit that owing to the confusion I have maintained I am the last person to decide whether any of it has taken a course toward good sense, or even usable ideas in that direction. Still, I am not where I started, I think.

What is a writer? What is an artist? How does the artist know that she has done art? What should the artist's focus be? To return to Tranströmer's "Codex," I omitted to look at the actual people represented in the poem. Take "Adam Ilebourgh 1448":

Who?
It was he who made the organ spread its clumpy wings and rise—
and it held itself airborne nearly a minute.
An experiment blessed with success!

So we know a little bit about Adam Ilebourgh, and it is possible to find out more. We will not discover much of anything that tells us more about Ilebourgh's art or his unsung contribution to that art. But we can extrapolate the possibility that without Ilebourgh's almost anonymous contribution, the next step (the step leading to Bach?) might not have happened, or might have evolved into an entirely different butterfly in the process of musical evolution.

That is what matters! It is good to read the masters of the past in their success: Homer, Sappho, Lucretius, Virgil, Du Fu, Chaucer, Shakespeare, Dickens, Whitman, Dickinson, Rossetti (Christina),

Twain, a list I make very quickly and pretty much arbitrarily, save that, for the first six writers, we have no idea what training they had in their art, and that for the last six, we know that they had no particular training; in fact, none of them either enjoyed or tolerated much formal education at all. Each of them might as well be anonymous (efforts continue to anonymize poor Shakespeare). What they left, they left. The rest of the tradition, almost all of the tradition, belongs to the written Codex. We belong to that Codex, but only insofar as we have done the work we know and think and strive to do. For itself.

*

I began all this with a more than slightly "mistake"-ridden quotation from Samuel Becket. The translation of that has been floating around for some time now, and it is beyond doubt that it has (poor Becket, who was, nevertheless, open to even the most feckless of ironies) become a cliché. But, as it has much to do with the subject here, it will not suffer from one more repetition:

"Ever tried. Ever failed. No matter. Try again. Fail again. Fail better."

*

I am going to finish (finally? finally!) by listening to some of us. I went back through last summer's edition of *Unstrung* in search of some more stammers, bent finger-prints, efforts that may or may not begin to succeed, but which fit into the Codex we have all been participating in all along. Each poet is among the youngest in that edition, and with one exception all the pieces are excerpts, unfairly perhaps but intentionally isolated. What, in fact and eventually is not an excerpt? Like Sappho, we are all made up of fragments, or else we are finished.

For the purpose of this exercise, I am not including the names of the poets, but with a little very and very appropriate effort you can find them in that edition of *Unstrung*. If you cheat and look, you fail in this; you will have missed the point (point?) of my wandering, and to quote G. B. Shaw and a very dear late friend, "The angels will weep for you." Or they will not.

*

Selenity Book Four

1
the shards of liquor bottles, guised
as stones, reflect the searing sunrays
of the afternoon.
glass that is now desert,
arranged like patches on a quilt.
each shard has a density
and hue; each shard is an emblem
carrying a history of tragedy &
jubilee.
bottles that Chicano boys drink
& throw into washes, bottles of
hard liquor consumed by Yaqui boys;
bottles that break like their reflections.
broken bottles like the memories
of drunken saguaros, who drink
sunrise and vomit ashes.
they are phantoms, who don't
know their names & who wait
for the rain to fill up the washes.
their gratitude is all this glass
on the bed of the wash,
an offering in return for
the liquor of grey skies.
a wash of desert glass is
a mirror made of these shards
reflecting the sun &
all the forgotten faces of Tucson.

2
"Do you bleed?"
I asked the bird
"Do you feel as I do?
I've suffered idleness
And so I must tell you
Of the dreams I have of endless seas
And of temples vandalized.

My love for you undying,
Yet still away you fly.
The sky may welcome you,
But my words a tempest make.
I will cage you in my chest
For I have no heart to break."

．　．　．

"Do you speak?"
I asked the mountain,
"Do you feel as I do?
Every drop of sweat
Was to become worthy of you.
Though I still have fear of falling
And being blinded by the sun,
I want only for my devotion
To set loose your crystal tongue.
My words are to you unmoving
For your roots run far too deep.
Without the strength to crush you,
You'll dissolve in tears I weep."

3
Sir,
You taught well—I admit.
To this day, words drop out of me:
Light . . . with pause, and
Fearful.
Because little girls shall not make large ripples
But you ripped much more than my voice.
So now I make a sound, Sir.
for every disregard,
every lie to match convenience,
every shove into the corners of my mind,
i thank you.
My mind is now furnished with the comforts of a home
that you never could provide

And a heart large enough for a world said to have no heart for me.
thank you.
for the cutting curses
that cut me free from the complacency of a life
meant to keep my head down
So that I could float above the world to a found home and
thank you
for beating me down until I didn't know myself
So that I had to stand up again to be found
and most importantly,
thank you
for hurting me
So I could learn to weigh importance with pain.
it hurts to look you in the eye, sir.
nowadays it hurts to look just about anyone in the eye.
because what you did to me was enough
to stop looking for anything in others.

4
Tell me why I should see your question mark
and do anything but take the hooked end and
hang you in the town square, ill omen that you are
vision of the silence you forced upon
me.
Tell me why it is because I still have the heart
to love the ones who left me guarding dying pumpkins.
Tell me why when question marks appear
my veins are lined with gunpowder,
this overly tied tongue's weak wick stands ready
the sticks of dynamite that pose as my corrupted skeleton
are whispering as they collide.
You stand with lighter in clenched yellow rose fist
flicking flame at my timidity like lashes of the devil's
tail.
And my eyes are glitching timers
trying to foresee their own destruction
and not comprehending why, WHY

a question
could so pose itself simply
but just dangerously enough to stand me on the
edge of infinity
and dare me to answer
with its 99 cent lighter inches from my fuse.

*

In the *Paris Review* interview, David Lehman asked A. R. Ammons, "Do you think poetry has any future?"

> Ammons replied, "It has as much future as past—very little."
>
> Lehman: "Could you elaborate on that?"
>
> Ammons: "Poetry is everlasting. It is not going away. But it has never occupied a sizable portion of the world's business and probably never will."

Reality is always good news, and this is reality. So is the work of the poets quoted above. So is our work.

Selenity Book Four

Anomalopoesis

After Wards: a Disconstruction of Future Reflection
Washington, late spring, 1864

walnut cabinet
rounded front
curved glass doors
confound
his way out of terror
four shelves laden with nostrums
most in gray-green gangrene tins
labels like all
language now partly ob
literated man
gled like words in ward

in silence, in dream's projection
raises eyes from unfol
ded letter
unwilling to move or see or
breathe
reads what can be seen of each row of tins

down
ward from shelf to shelf to shelf to shelf
word-lorn tally athwart this days deaths
gawks into a specter of his pallor in the curve of glass

	ACCIDIUM		SMITHI		YLUM	
	TANNICUM		NTRAS			
ARB.		ASSI		CII		LACTOSUM
		IDIUM		PHAS		
	SODII		SINAPIS	M	IS	
	BORAS	ALBA			AS	
OTASSI FT.			FLDEXT	CCARINUM		
OD TART.			RGOT			
		INCI		IACTOSUM		
		DUM				

>>>

Walt sorts sheaf of un
folded letters
puts several unread into pocket
to read later by him

self

maybe over and

over
again

to no one anymore

returns to ward
tired
bonebonebone
bonetired

and hearty grieved
a grievous day

and oh wordless word
less word less
as a photograph of night

O
beautiful

be persuaded*

*In the constructed future reflection: "(Come sweet death! be persuaded, O beautiful death!)"

Selenity Book Four

Note to the Office of Interpretation
Nick Salerno,
Magister Ludi

I am delivering the enclosed ideas to you,
four of them so far, maybe five.
I anticipate that each of the ideas
is connected to the other three, or four.

I will not bore you trying to explain the connection
even if I thought myself worthy to do so.
Besides, each idea will explain at least part
of one or more or all of the other ideas.

The first idea is the trillium
       alone under a dying aspen.
The second idea is that morning in April that rose
       like a yellow cactus blossom over the bay in Guaymas.
The third idea is a knot in a pine wall, the one just above
       the homely lamp made of a cholla skeleton.
The fourth idea is what we just saw run out of
       the screen door letting it slam, as usual.

One idea can never stand alone, so you say.
But if one idea *must* be supported
by at least one other idea, in their mutual support
they may speak only to one another, like poet to poet,
       player to player, soul to soul.

And finally to anyone outside cloister or workshop
welcome to a sense of new ideas. Inside scholastic cryptophilia,
whatever *is* is only another pebble to kneel on, to prove
the breathless scruples of the lapidary imagination.

But outside! Ah.
Yes, there is a fifth idea.
Just there. And there as well. That multiplex world,
everywhere you and I have spoken.

What is seems

always to be and be and solid—
No No No!
Not always!

All that is always is never
all ways but not all ways never either
neither of which may (may not)

exist (!)
seems always to be—seems—
love—

like
"Love, Nickie" or
"Love, Dickie"—
pudgy valedictions, silly, age-old, respectable

is
being love actually but always. For us
always for the same reason
is love
*

The young mother
in the row of seats in front of me
here in the dentist's waiting (always waiting)
room

reads to the blond toddler on her lap,
Words. And pictures readable only by her child
about the Tooth Fairy.
Close attention as palliative. Daddy texts.
*

> > >

Selenity Book Four

It is not the catalogue of memories we long for
but the real, solid and whole person we demand—

even knowing that whatever is real, solid and whole
ever was the unreal, dissolved and unwholesome

in *ourselves* that we grieve
and not the contents of the urn closeted somewhere

real, solid in each discrete particle of ash
and as whole as the image of smoke can be whole.

Lines Too Lonely to Find their Poem
an *Election Year Confession from the Lost Percent*

In the shadow of the table of the feast of living,
we can't even ask for the salt.
               No one will hear us.

Salt isn't good for us anyway.
              *

I have plenty of room on that bench for my hat.
              No one is near me.

The soft touch of a warm hand might awaken the heartbeat
              I have learned never to dance to.
              *

I do not have to earn anyone's respect.

If I am noticed at all it is to hear behind my back in clanging noise
      that is irresistible to my longing
      for the painful music of words,
            that I do not need respect.

Respect might inflate what is left of the fading lorn shadow
      of pride that I never learned to deserve.
              *

So I am done with the bell and music of the skeletal voice
        I have stumbled toward the bankrupt edges of a long life.
I am invited to fade from the illusion of life I was wrong to think
        had been advanced to my fair account.
              *

We stand behind the unwashable glass of our race,
      or we lie on the consciousness of angry bedsores,
      or sit in the shadow of the doorway to shadow,

                                                        > > >

Selenity Book Four

      sprawl in the cosmic fuzz of drugs, drink,
           the contorted succor of delirium.
              *

If we were ever cursed by visibility we might be allowed to believe
      that we chose this candle-end of life.

We beg ourselves to allow that our colors are no one's fault but our own.
      It is our sign to the attentive world that we prefer
           to be thrust aside.
              *

The bed, the wheelchair,
      the isolated kingdom of an ill-featured mind
      locked within the broken doll of a soul.

Or the broken tendrils of the otherness of love
      requited by beatings and public infamy.

All our fault and our doing or our parents'
      or the cold inevitable caress of genetics.
           *

We should declare this loneliness to be a blessed state.

We are relieved of the perils of responsibility,
      the anguish of fulfilling grief,
      the public discomforts of wisdom,
      the creative pain of love.

And the silence we have earned instead is the silence
      of the affliction of age,
      of angry and speechless dotage,
           the improvident wisdom of senility.
              *

> > >

Still, my collaborative heart will pound beyond its time,
        beyond the decay of senses,
              the feast of living.

The abandoned heart thrums in silent bloodless spasms.

The shadow of immortality shuffles like another disease,
        leprous and sacred

infusing for the wealthy of nations its holy meal
        of my unmarked
              lime-salted corpse
                    or raw ash for desert and dessert.

Selenity Book Four

Families on Streets in Cities

The family on Elm Street here in Madison
moved out very suddenly. The neighbor
between us told me that they had lost their home
to Chase, or some other bank. She was a teacher.
He worked at a bank. Not Chase, I don't think.
I did not know them. I think they had kids.

The family on Locust Avenue here in Reading
moved out very suddenly. The neighbor
between us told me that they had lost their home
to B of A, or some other bank. She was a teacher.
He worked at a bank. Not B of A, I don't think.
I did not know them. I think they had kids.

The family on Sycamore Drive here in Silverton
moved out very suddenly. The neighbor
between us told me that they had lost their home
to Wells Fargo, or some other bank. She was a teacher.
He worked at a bank. Not Wells Fargo, I don't think.
I did not know them. I think they had kids.

The family on Palm Lane here in Riverside
moved out very suddenly. The neighbor
between us told me that they had lost their home
to Citigroup, or some other bank. She was a teacher.
He worked at a bank. Not Citigroup, I don't think.
I did not know them. I think they had kids.

The families lived on streets and avenues
and drives and lanes. They had neighbors.
They lost their homes to banks, none of which
he worked for, so far as any of us know.
She was a teacher. We think they had kids.
I Google Zillow listings in their towns.

> > >

I am beginning to want to know them,
and I think I would walk down the street
to visit. But it is too late. I get those robo-calls.
Flyers from outfits that will pay cash, quick,
for my house. Sight almost unseen. Guaranteed.
Vacant houses bought by rental outfits. You too?

The neighbor who told me about them is moving out.

Selenity Book Four

Alice among the Wonders

This morning she left her apartment or her rental house.
She set off to find the Job Providers she recognizes
by the cut of the backs of their suits. The tailored strut.

Alice scours Milwaukee* for the Door to the Good Provider.
Meanwhile, frumious paws, black-gloved, toss her belongings
out onto the street, almost as fast as snatching claws

had already changed her lock. Then the belongings
that don't belong anymore are picked through.
Vanishing Alices watch backs turn and desert.

On the curb, what used to belong to any Alice is sold
to the next Alice to be evicted in some tenement
up or down the street. Which street? Which address?

Alices' addresses may have mattered once, to Alices.
Streets rot into hollow alleys that blacken into tunnels.
Alices in tunnels grope among dark sparks of lies.

Gray shadows of Alices gather in the dust of
their American nightmare. Alices cry for comfort
outside the stylish barrens of an unspeakable New World.

For the full adventure, read Evicted: Poverty and Profit in an American City *by Matthew Desmond (Crown 2016). Consider the city—cities, really—of your choice, or the sadness of your own cruel dependence, in or out of the barrens.*

La Plume d'Anthropocène

In the last few years,
turns of the seasons,
the fashion seasons
dans le monde paleontologique,

the dinosaurs have been groomed
with the softness of feathers,
even to the lucid dreams of designs
in avian color, titanium sheen of starlings.

So sudden!
Dinosaurs are dressed
for the latest fashion in ornate
patterns of immaculate extinction.

Yet we of the mammalian
generic *Anthropos* struggle to evolve
at the pace of dead trilobites.
Our plumage remains invisible.

Our footprints stain Earth in drying red.
We evolve so slowly, save downward
toward the lowly dust
of our sere demise.

Still,
extinction is no disgrace.

The end is quick, sepulchered
into the slow evolution of memorial agate.
We grow beautiful and virtuous again
all together in the same lithic kiln.

Selenity Book Four

Lych-Gathering

Protecting her young of some species,
a mother at the beach leaves the corpses of biting flies
scattered on a deck beneath her.

Wistless-like I wish for the ghost of Matthew Brady,
the ghost and the ghost's chimerical camera,
the worthy who might render annihilation

in the iron bas-relief photogravure
and proto-gravitas,
lines

of blackened corpses swept off
the deck, sinking
Styxward into the obsidian depths.

The dead remain remembered only
in the media-driven catafalque below headlines,
the legacy of passing insult.

The species turns almost human, the mother,
the young, the flies. But first and finally
we all tumble and rust into the cold magic of glass plates.

Surprise, Surprise

She peers out from the chainlinkfence of her mind.
Peers out at the cloudless blue sky
she and her family purchased away from the
other neighborhood. The Others.

And, a gift of Surprise, the gated entrance
and the security of HOA and
more than a few guns locked securely
about the sacred corona of household—

Looks out at that blue sky,
cloudless, save for a little brown this morning.
The brown will clear off after the rush hour.
A little.

She straightens and presses
her detergent-washed and whiter-
than-white Ajaxed neighborhood
security vocabulary, and she turns
to face now the Boys and Girls Club

that will not happen, must not happen
because of the laundered caution she will
instill in her offspring and heirs,
and John's and the neighbors,
the right and correct neighbors' Children of Light.

Her thoughts spill out and out
bronzed in polished entrepreneurial sureness:
goodmoralvalues   goodworkethic
honestyandintegrity   myprivilegedwhitekid

a bulwark of good values set against:
a community infiltrated with AT-RISK children who may
offer the wrong kind of examples.   >>>

Selenity Book Four

There are offers that we will not consider
among the offers we will accept:

a neighborhood that is oneofthemostbeautifulinthecity—
a revampedparkwithmorewalkingtrails,
a beautificationprocessthatmustn'tmustn'tbeimpeded
by scampsandurchinswhowilldeterfutureresidents
frombuyinghomes

But Boys and Girls club kids will roam
and rummage through our pride of concern:
Safety. Security. Freedom of unimpeded enterprise
and property values not shared by the Others
from the old neighborhoods. The Them.

But noillfeelings about their:
brokenhomes   atriskchildren   wrongwrongwrong
wrongkindofexample   outsideteens
Teens Roaming the Community UNSUPERVISED!   UN!!!

Oh my privileged white kid! My child and my shadow!
She looks again into the blue.
Breathes a purchased breath in the freedom of brown-tinged air,
coughs, just a little, feels the rasp, just a little.

Breathes out what she can of the brown-tinged
atmosphere of her fears,
exhales what is left of the illfeelings
she does not have
wouldneversomuchasentertainforaminute

and wonders if the chainlink gate
of the chainlink mind will have room
for just one more insignificant little padlock.

>>>

She heaves a proprietary sigh,
breathes a proprietary lungful of her private oxygen,
turns and ushers her dominion of blue
blue sky—picturesquely tinged with the morning's
Surprise of Sonoran beige—
inside where she can't see either color, anycoloranymore.

She turns the AC way down to warm her soul
and draws the curtains and waits for Them to build—

Ah! That Wall*

*The words run together are bits of statements made by residents of the Arizona city, Surprise, on the subject of their rejecting a Boys and Girls Club in the area. I ran them together, or they ran themselves together, to indicate that they are noises behind which no thought exists, but which reflect the residents' state of "mind." I am hoping that the jumble will ask my readers to untangle the mess in order to contemplate the appalling bigotry that we are so accustomed to that we often fail to notice it, even, or especially, when it is coming from our own heads.

Selenity Book Four

Anomalopoesis: whiffs of a morning with *Garbage*

poetry . . . / reaches down into the dead pit / . . .
and / brings up hauls of stringy gook which it arrays /
with light and strings of shiny syllables . . . /
but of course, there / is some untransformed material,
namely the poem / itself . . .
    A. R. Ammons, "Garbage," part 17

The gods created things—
stuff, animal, vegetable, the us.
The noun, the fallen,

fell, felled, the fell blow, fell words
fallen from lexical offal,
all sluffed off fortunate lies of fell innocence.

We created the connections,
the movings about, the verb.
And the slosh of movement: sex.

Lucretius is Rome's little joke on the Middle Ages:
the Middle Ages of the Middle Ages
and the Middle Ages of Now.

To Lucretius
what does matter matter?
All's matter, and there's no matter.

Some matter matters
just enough for what we regard as Poetry,
as the poetry that reminds us that

beauty: all that is impossible,
all abstractions,
(well, beautiful or not, but beautiful)

> > >

because the artist's job is not to draw you into nature;
it is to draw you out of nature into yourself
and bring nature with you anew.

Beauty is also made up of atoms,
or might as well be.
Blessed unreality is also a solid chunk of atoms.

Smoke rises
dissipates into what matters.
What matters is.

The goal of poetry is to announce the stunned and hushed
Eureka! of silence.
You hear this from me. You will not see it modeled in me.

We have words for the flash of unspeakable
dark before the speakable Nothingness, nothingless.
We have no word though for Nothingness.

We have a word for the infinitesimal spot of time
between life and nothingness.
We have yet to invent a word for death.

Orphans in Concordia

1
Ed: Well, he was always [
                ] tractor. The first time [

Ivan:] [

Mrs. Ed: [*laughs*]

Ed:]coon huntin' [
                ]first rifle. A little [
                ]coon just sat there in the branch

Mrs. Ed: *laughs again, as always [?]*

Ed: Well
                Best time to grow up in anyway

2
The Orphan Train Museum squats
behind a *bas relief* steam engine,
brown on the side wall.

The engine skews at an angle forward
obliquely to plow into oncoming traffic
like the locomotive in that first disaster film

blackandwhite and silent as the Screams
in the bleeding (blackandwhite) audience,
one century's iron into another century's alloys and plastic.

> > >

3
Ed and Ivan and Ed's Wife
> *Sorry. Ed and Ivan never mentioned your name.*
> *We have so many kinds of orphans these days.*
> *Names. Words. Whole identities.*
rise in age-appropriate modulated grace.

Ed bids good-bye.
Aims toward the parking lot.

Ivan and Ivan's Wife look after Ed.
They seem not so sure which direction Ed
has decided on,

if he's decided, even after he's headed
in the mis-direction something decided him on.
Decided, for Ed and themselves,

Ed's memory being yet another orphan.
Old age orphans us all.
Ivan and Ivan's Wife open the door and go out it.

4
"I think you drop'd something."

Could be another member of Ed's family.
Same largeness, and gray. Same Kansas.

I don't see what he picks up.
"I know it wasn't yours," he adds.
"I guess I'm just another picker-upper; don't want anyone to slip."

> > >

5
Orphan.
From Greek, "orphanos,"
"bereaved."

For Ed and Mrs. Ed and Ivan and Concordia
I am bereaved.
And alone.

I dream again and again and again of the black engines
of my earliest orphan's
westward horizon.

Notes from M. Arouet

Life is fleeting.
Life is short and life is insignificant.

When we write to the dead,
we write also to all of history and not *from* history,

and so far as we are able
we write to all of memory.

Memory is living beyond living
(such a dull statement!)

We write on behalf of what will always be un-remembered and re-created.

The respect we owe to the living is our lending them the chance and challenge
        of remembering along with us—

and joining the,
    well,
           responsibilities:
            *

The poet is responsible to the past for the past.
The poet is responsible for the entirety of human past behind past,

of human present and human future—
as witness, as scholar, as, if not sage, patient interlocutor.

It falls to the recorder of what is human to extend
to the human dominion as well—
        each individual, human or not.
          *

                                              > > >

It is a trap of course,
the exit from which is the poet's other responsibility,
that the poet writes—

speaks, sings, prays, laments on words outside words—
to each individual to whom the poet is responsible.
The poet is free to listen back in turn.

Tourist as Shaman/Shaman as Tourist
(Kartchner Caverns)

Of course you need to leave your mark here,
a sacred handprint in a sacred place.
How can you leave Underworld by merely leaving?

Clap your souvenir cap to your head and go?
Grab a pre-wrapped sandwich
before you squint your way to the parking lot?

At the very least you need to touch the damp living wall
with your warm hand, *need* to
feel the cool. But you shiver and refrain.

Better that you let the cool touch bless the rest of you
with your sense of eons in this holy undercroft.
Merely to touch may leave no mark.

To touch merely, to be touched merely
will leave a shared emblem on you
and on the shadow-wall of the cave.

But you also know about purity.
How easily purity is contaminated.
How easily you may be contaminated.

You keep your wanting, grieving hand in its pocket.
Feeling your hand there, maybe touching nothing
but the familiar car keys, your grandfather's pocket knife,

you know in your fingers, whatever they touch,
that they touch whatever mark you have left,
what mark you have been left with.

You share, not touching the generations
you have been touched by,
that you touch.

Selenity Book Four

Ending After Wards: Continuing a Disconstruction of Future Reflection
Washington, late spring, 1864

cabinet
front
doors
confound
out of terror
nostrums
gangrene tins
all
obliterated
words in ward

dream's projection
unfolded letter
to move or see or
the
row of tins

to shelf
athwart this days deaths
pallor in the curve of glass

```
          UM              I                   UM
          UM              AS

B.                I                   II          SUM
                  UM                  AS

          II              IS    M     S
          AS      A                         S

FT.               EXT           UM
ART.              OT

                  CI            SUM
                  M
                                                        >>>
```

unfolded letters

unread into pocket
by himself

and

over
again

more

to ward
red
bone
red

grieved
day

less word
less
night

O
ful

suaded*

*In the constructed future reflection: "(Come sweet death! be persuaded, O beautiful death!)"

Selenity Book Four

Break: Selene Eos

Måne

On a few July evenings then the moon has a nose.
Not a mere man-in-the-moon shadow
of long aped dull fantasy, but the real thing, drawn
smack in the middle of that mythic dead face.

But the moon has a nose only for a few minutes
on these few July evenings, before the moon rises
to bridesmaid pinks or oranges of evening glow.
We admit we knew, and know

even on that first show as the moon rose
into its expected late day grayness, that the moon,
the dead man, will leave its nose behind,
just above the distant tree line. Then someday

we will see again what we have seen all these July evenings,
determined against our rude intrusions of reason,
to forget for only those days that the nose was only
the sparse top of an ancient dying jack pine,

standing at some inexplicable distance across the lake,
a decrepit tree whose distant great length
is still overtaking its dusk-coal gray Jurassic head
in some primordial ritual of starvation.

We will also admit our glad failure to find that pine
on each of those eschatological July days.
We drove along country dirt roads. We peeled our eyes
for coordinates among sunlight, road, and direction,

nature, invention, philosophy appropriately blended,
to reveal the actual artifact of mere tree.
We knew and we know we needn't hurry.
Even dying, even still, the jack pine may well outlast us.

> > >

But of all the creatures in this summer pantomime,
the unfeatured moon is neither dying nor searching.
In our own dying and searching we will look up into the pines
and see the moon's nose from our grounded humanness,

or we will not. Turning any corner we choose
on this country dirt road, what matters to the moon,
or the pine, or to us, after all, may be merely our looking,
and looking together—at imaginary features in a solid dream,

at a rock-face in a desert sun, directed by impervious lines,
articulate isness perfectly blended into the script of eons of erosion.
Characters too immediate to the soul for mere beauty.
A shaman-world of necessary generation—that abundance.

The apposite ideal of what the pencil and eraser will do
like a ghost to erode the sheet of paper that reflects
the scratches of the written poem—a grave-rubbed moon-face
that cannot erase itself from lives that must be erased,

that, like even the moon, will do nothing else.

Selenity Book Four

Endnotes to "A Case for the Lonely Poet"

[i] Samuel Beckett, *Worstward Ho*.

[ii] William Stafford's phrase. It is usefully corrective to vanity and other symptoms of panic.

[iii] Interviewed by David Lehman in *The Paris Review*, summer 1996.

[iv] One of the very few poets in the 2014 *Best of American Poetry* not aligned with the profession is Sean Thomas Dougherty, who works in a pool hall and tutors private students.

[v] "Poetry Slam or, the decline of American Verse," *Harper's*, July 2013.

[vi] Werner Herzog, *The Cave of Forgotten Dreams*.

[vii] University of Chicago Press, 1968.

[viii] Do I really need to identify this?

[ix] *The Complete Poems of Emily Dickinson*, Thomas Johnson, ed.

[x] Guy Davenport, trans. in *The Norton Book of Classical Literature*. At the time of writing, I do not have access to Ann Carson's translation, which I would have quoted from. But this'll do for now.

[xi] Anne Carson, trans. "Fragment 67a" from *If Not, Winter: Fragments of Sappho*. Vintage 2002.

[xii] Susan Howe, *My Emily Dickinson*, p. 22.

[xiii] *ibid.* p. 23.

[xiv] A. R. Ammons, *Sphere*, p. 16 (section 13).

[xv] R. F. S. "Respiration," from *Disordinary Light*.

www.ingramcontent.com/pod-product-compliance
Lightning Source LLC
Chambersburg PA
CBHW020905090426
42736CB00008B/498